Kirsten Luckins' first collection, *The Trouble With Compassion*, was published by Burning Eye in 2(Festival. She wrote and toured al show to accompany it, the secor written with ACE support. Her fir *Stolen*, came second in the 2014 Show.

C000219344

Kirsten blogs at kirstenluckins.worupicss.com. on Twitter @ImesldaSays, or on Instagram for illustration projects @imelda_says

Utterly Otterly

KIRSTEN LUCKINS

This edition published by Bx3
an imprint of Burning Eye Books
2017

Burning Eye Books
15 West Hill, Portishead, BS20 6LG

ISBN 978-1-911570-33-2

For otter-lovers everywhere

CONTENTS

INTRODUCTION

In April 2016, I took part in the collective mayhem that is NaPoWriMo – National Poetry Writing Month. Poets all over the globe log on every day for a new writing prompt, dash off a poem and post their efforts on blogs or in Facebook groups.

Every day in April.

That's thirty poems in all.

Up until then, I'd never made it past fourteen. I'd always hit a wall, usually when my fancy remained untickled by one of the official prompts. So I said I'd try again, only this time with an extra rule of my own…

…every poem MUST feature an otter.

I swear I was only joking.

DAY ONE

Write a lune – a poem where every verse has three lines,
organised with five–three–five words per line.

To fully appreciate my lune, please look up the video of 'otters
playing free jazz on a Casio' on your favourite interweb device.
Trust me.

OTTERS PLAYING FREE JAZZ ON A CASIO

'How do you approach playing
with otters in
the absence of chord changes?

How do you even begin?'
asks JazzAcademy.com's homepage,
neglecting to ask these otters:

GET HOT! Kitten neeeeeds keys,
ain't no baloney,
we   AB   SO   LUTE   LY

hip to the short-clawed jive,
gotsa screaming meemies,
we collective, daddy-o, we radicaliiiiiiiiised!

DAY TWO

Write about a family photograph.

I wasn't too keen on this prompt, and for a moment feared I might fall at the first hurdle. Or rather the second hurdle, if this is an analogy where prompts are hurdles, but anyway you know what I mean and I digress.

I was saved by Husband asking me, in the dead of night, whilst shaking with barely-suppressed laughter –

'What if otters were potters?'

What indeed.

OTTERS OF THE WORLD, UNITE!

Answer me this – what if otters were potters?
Would living by water make their clay wetter?
Would they throw sloppy pots that all teeter and totter?
Would holding down splatter make pots a lot squatter?
Surely it follows their kilns should burn hotter?
So they must buy their wood from a local woodcutter
(wood-burning kilns being certainly better
to use than electric, when potting near water).

But what if the cutter bamboozles the otters,
never once offering wood on a platter,
but ripping them off with some shitty sales patter?
Thus lining his pockets, the cutter gets fatter,
whilst, locked into poverty, knocked on their uppers,
the lot of the otters just never gets better!
Will the otters not notice that something's the matter?
Will discontent not sound its note in their natter?!
Revolt and rise up, oh you downtrodden otters!
Even fat cutters need pots made by potters!
TEAR DOWN THE KILN-WOOD-MONOPOLY ROTTERS!

Don't look at me like I'm some kind of nutter.

DAY THREE

Write a love letter, or fan mail.

In 2012, the then-Mayor of London, Boris Johnson, wrote a column for the Telegraph newspaper, commenting on the Olympic Games then being held in his city. In it, he said this:

> *As I write these words, semi-naked women are playing volleyball in the Horseguards Parade immortalised by Canaletto. They are glistening like wet otters, as the rain plashes from the brims of the spectators' sou'westers.*

From that one quote, you may be able to draw many conclusions about Mr Johnson's educational and class background, about his attitude towards female Olympic athletes and, by extension, women in general, but...

...what I saw was his terrifying ignorance of Japanese folklore!

For the Japanese know that otters do indeed shapeshift into the forms of beautiful women, in order to seduce, kill and *eat men just like Boris*!

Here then, is a love letter from some imaginary Japanese shapeshifting, man-eating, volleyball-playing otters to the Right Honourable Boris Johnson. In honour of Japanese culture, it is of course a series of linked haiku.

BORIS JOHNSON AND THE OTTERS

Sexy otter girls,
sleek! You watch, Borisu-san,
but do not see we.

Silly! We see you
feast eyes on we lissom limbs,
silken like tofu.

Suave you phrases plash!
Rain from you lyrical tongue!
Favourite muscle!

Storehouse of treasure,
you brain sleep in marrow sea,
soft, sashimi-grade.

Speak we of art now?
Great man, stories of great men!
You hair *kawaiiiii!*[1]

Shall we little claws
scratch you noble shoulders, broad
like Kobe beef-cow?

Secret, we sharp teeth
wait for you, *ichiban*[2] man,
steamy bean dumpling!

Shhhhh! You no mind knives.
We whet them in you honour,
delicious *Borisu-san...*

---

1   cute
2   number one

DAY FOUR

**Is April the cruellest month, as TS Eliot would have us believe?
Write about the cruelty of other months.**

I took this instruction very seriously, embarking on literal minutes of research, during which I found out many things about recorded otter deaths plotted on graphs on a month-by-month basis.

It didn't spark a poem.

However, did you know that, on the Native American zodiac, each astrological sign is reassigned to a totem animal? Thus 'Aquarius' becomes – you guessed it – 'Otter'!

Joy.

WHAT MONTH IS WORST FOR OTTERS?

'Oh, wow, that's a hard one, isn't it, babe? I mean, speaking as an Otter, I suppose I'd have to say late Jan, early Feb, just because of the flooding we've been getting? Which is totally ironic, because that's our birth month, so it's sort of like our power month? But then, like Gary says, I really showed my creative spirit last year when I dug in the fourth exit *above* flood level, he says that's pure Otter, you know, because we're, like, inventors? And I made sure it opens to the north, which you know is our spirit direction? So I guess maybe I'd say August, September time, partly 'cause the pups are off by then and I get a bit of empty-holt syndrome, don't I, babe? But mainly I think it's just that time of year is all about Bear, and that's not great for me, 'cause you know I used to work for a Bear and she was just so fussy and uptight and expected everyone to work the whole time and all she wore was brown, like *literally* all the time, and you know the whole thing about her being my natural predator made for a bit of stress in the workplace, so I had to leave in the end? I used to call her un-Bear-able, didn't I, babe? Didn't I? Call her un-Bear-able? Oh yeah, me and Gary are both Otters, so are the pups. Except Jamie, she's a Woodpecker?

Not sure how that happened?'

DAY FIVE

Incorporate names of heritage breed vegetables into your poem.

Yeah, so otters have very little time for heritage vegetable breeds, even though I did find out about a zoo that feeds veggies to its otters by concealing them in sushi. I wanted to write a love song for Husband, who at the time was having some anxiety issues. Do you know that sea otters sleep holding hands?

ASSESSING MY SIGNIFICANT OTTER

When she asked me to describe you,
I could have said
the North Sea to a fishtank
is his heart to this small, bland room.

When she asked what she had missed,
I could have said
there is a tangle of black razorwire deep down;
can he unspool it safely
in this neutral room?

When she asked me how this is affecting us,
I could have said
he calls me to the window to watch the goldfinches;
when we sleep we hold hands like otters,
so we never drift apart.

DAY SIX

Explore your relationship with food.

This caused a small tizz in my head. Surely they mean 'explore an otter's relationship with food'? But there are so many species! Thirteen! Thirteen species of otters! And they all eat slightly different things! Should I write about Japanese otters keeping paddy fields free of crayfish? Or giant Amazonian otters being slowly poisoned by mercury from gold ore extraction accumulated in the livers of their favourite fish? These are questions I would never have had to ask myself if I hadn't started this ridiculous challenge!

Instead I wrote a happy little Winnie-the-Pooh-esque ditty about the masters of the tummy buffet, the Californian sea otter. They need to eat a quarter of their body weight every day to keep them warm in the seas off northern California. And they love abalone.

THE HAPPY FEEDING SONG OF THE SEA OTTER

Floating along on my own-e-o,
Smashing my abalone-e-o,
On my smashing stone-e-o,
I go whack! whack! whack!

Don't ever cook it with po-tay-ter,
Celery, soy sauce, or a to-may-ter,
Don't gratinise it with a cheese gray-ter,
I just knock! it! back!

DAY SEVEN

Write a tritina.

Which is like half a sestina: three verses that end their lines with the same three words, in different orders.

As my subject, I chose the Korean folk saying that a person who sees an otter will always bring rain wherever they go.

THE CURSE OF THE KOREAN OTTER

I have seen an otter, and lost the sun.
From this day, I will always draw the clouds
to trail me, black and faithful as a dog.

I swear, at first I thought it was a dog
trotting through the long grass in the sun.
I called to it. My call became a cloud.

The callous skies are thickening with cloud,
and where I walk it's raining cats and dogs.
At night I dream of basking in the sun,

but when the sunrise comes, I'm dogged by clouds.

DAY EIGHT

Write about a flower.

Otters have no use for flowers. Can't eat 'em, juggle 'em, or slide down 'em. But if you put 'flower' and 'otter' into a search engine of your choice[3] you too may encounter the charming fashion blog of the Modern Otter, who has a thing or two to say about floral prints, yes he does. What an inspirational chap.

---

3   Alternatively, you could go straight to www. themodernotter.com

THE MODERN OTTER

The modern otter is not afraid of florals.
The modern otter has thrown away his plaid.
An avid consumer of articles sartorial,
He's nine parts hipster to one part lad.

The modern otter tries some unexpected chinos,
Balancing the flower print with simple chambray.
He dreams of days in Paris sipping stylish cappuccinos.
The modern otter hankers for a stroll along the Seine.

Transitioning to spring wear in optimistic camel,
Pairing it with indigo, or black, or dusty blues,
He folds a natty turn-up in his nethermost apparel,
His naked ankles shiver over waterproof dress shoes.

The modern otter favours crisply pointed collars,
Longs for you to notice, but he's too safe to be seen.
And though the modern otter does eschew the brighter colours,
Occasionally he'll venture out in something hunter green.

DAY NINE

Write something that is scary or uncomfortable to say.

There's a phobia for everything, and the fear of otters is called lutraphobia. For this prompt I imagined delving into the mind of a wild swimming enthusiast who had developed lutraphobia whilst doing the breaststroke in the waters of the Upper Tyne.

I'll grant you, it's a complicated backstory for what is essentially a Wordsworthian, generic Romantic pastiche, but you have to understand that we're nine days in at this point and it's quite possible I'm starting to unravel slightly...

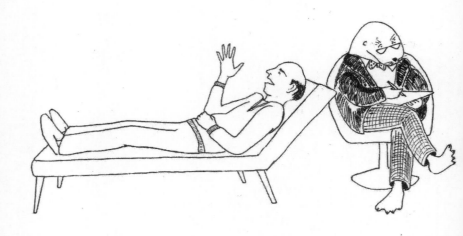

WILD SWIMMER'S LUTRAPHOBIA

I have oft-times swum delighted
       in the Tyne's electric cool
and wild waters, those summer eves
       in Corbridge's genteel lea.
I have eschewed pools municipal,
       crowded echo-chambers,
named them no better than aquaria,
       where captive mustelids might twirl
to the cooing of the crowd,
       their stank spray festering the public
air as rank as rotten fish.
       Those same aquatic weasels now
have barred me from my bliss,
       ruined all my joy in open water.
I cannot pinch the moment when
       the fear of them first grew upon me,
but now the chance whisk
       of waterweed at my floating wrist
casts trembles thro' my traitor limbs.
       Unbidden, images of muzzles poised
to crunch through hapless knuckles
       darken all my vision.
Too often I have seen, or thought I saw,
       these denizens slink
from their sandy twilit caves.
       Alas! the o'ershadowing doom
descends upon me, and I seek
       in swelling terror for paw print
or foul spraint upon my favoured shore,
       and though my mouth forms,
continual, a wavering O, yet never can I utter
       the name of my tormentor,
the dreadful title – OTTER!

DAY TEN

Write a list poem from the titles of books on your shelf.

Wow, you can tell day ten was a Sunday, can't you? Please feel free to add your own disgraceful otter puns to my poem. Seriously, write on the book and everything.

AN OTTER'S BOOKSHELF

Far From the Madding Otters
A Farewell to Otters
The Unbearable Lightness of Otters
The Otters of Wrath
The Otter Is a Lonely Hunter
The Girl with the Otter Tattoo
Fear and Otters in Las Vegas
For Whom the Otter Tolls
All's Quiet on the Otter Front
His Dark Otters trilogy
I Know Why the Caged Otter Squeaks
No Country for Old Otters
Of Otters and Men
Tender Is the Otter
The Otter of the Baskervilles
The Maltese Otter
Otters Are Not the Only Fruit
My Family and Otter Animals
All the Harry Otters, obviously
Tarka the Otter
The Shellfish Gene (bit of non-fiction there)
Salmon Fishing in the Yemen
Moby Dick (horror section)
Ring of Bright Water (horror section)
So Long and Thanks for All the Fish

DAY ELEVEN

Using James Wright's poem 'Lying in a Hammock at William Duffy's Farm in Pine Island, Minnesota' as an example, write a poem that describes a place, then ends with a philosophical statement.

My inspiration came from a nearby garden, which has always gladdened me with its huge array of unapologetically naff garden ornaments. The crowning glory is a stone-effect cast resin otter.

OTTERS AT THE BOTTOM OF THE GARDEN

This simple bench, back against
the pebble dash, is a trap for sun
on which I sit, patient as bait.
In the eaves a host of starlings
whirr, click and chuff, discordant
choristers for a strange faith.
A road may be inferred beyond
the horizon of the garden wall,
from the odd passages of cars.
In their wake a sucking, slapping,
almost entirely irregular boom.
I believe it is high tide. Yes, yes,
the bells of St Hilda's nod agreement.
A stray beam of April illuminates
the pocket lawn, cabochon emerald,
margins as dense with critters
as a mediaeval Book of Hours.
Gargoyles and dwarves wink plastic eyes
under the scrollwork of the hostas.
Amid bluebells, a goose gawps upwards,
its white throat a column of greed,
twice the height of a nearby flamingo.
And at my feet, resplendent,
scampers the *pièce de résistance* –
the moulded-resin, stone-effect,
not-quite-life-sized otter, apogee
of all that is good and pleasing.

It is not to have what you want,
but to want what you have
that is true happiness.

DAY TWELVE

Write a poem based on terms found in the index of a specialist manual, textbook or encyclopaedia.

Not having anything pertinent to marine biology just lying around, nor able to find anything in my local library, I was thrown on the mercy of the *Trawlermen's Handbook*. Luckily for me, commercial fishing vessels make use of 'otter boards' to direct their catch into their nets – you learn all kinds of things, don't you?

Otter Boards divert water flow into your nets.
Keep your Otter Boards well-adjusted.
They are boards for water, but not waterboards.

Please do not waterboard your otter,
they can hold their breath for four minutes,
at best you will merely annoy them,
and then you must quickly calculate
the Angle of Attack, which is the distance between your Otter Board
and the Direction of Flow,
calculated in degrees,
multiplied by your otter's annoyance.

If your otter shows a V-shape when sideways, it is a British otter
and remembers Agincourt.

If a piratical otter boards your vessel, repel!
Protect your salmon!
Otters may become unstable in the presence of large quantities
of salmon.

Stop your otter tilting by shortening their Upper and Lower Back-
strops accordingly. Careful of your fingers! They may strop back!

If you see your otter heeling inwards
and then heeling outwards, he has begun
his ritual dance of Saluting the Salmon,
and your catch is lost to you.
You should have repelled him when I told you to.

DAY THIRTEEN

Write a poem inspired by a fortune cookie motto.

Poking about online, I found a site dedicated to cookie mottos, including this implausibly long but entirely appropriate fortune:

Hidden in a valley beside an open stream – this will be the type of place where you will find your dream

It reminded me of a story my lovely friend Lilly told me. She was walking her dog on the banks of the river behind her house, when she saw an otter floating on its back in the water, for all the world looking like it was daydreaming. Lilly was convinced the otter was imagining its future mate and family, and behold! Some months later she saw the otter again, this time playing with two pups. They were on the opposite bank, and had found a red ball, which they were rolling to one another.

LILLY'S DREAMING OTTER

She dandles herself in the current
with her drowsy webfoot flutter,
all whiskery contentment,
she is *dolce fa niente*.
Upriver and down,
fishing and floating,
water and air,
balance in her belly and her heart.

She watches the wind sift the sky
into its several selves;
nested clouds, ribbons, tufts,
some dark enough to cry themselves
back into the slippery sheets
of her water-bed, this river
where she is dreaming up
a spry dog,
a glinty rogue,
a playmate.

They will make a home
where the river bank is scalloped
with beaches of pelt-brown sand.
They will make pups, a proper romp,
nose to tail to nose to tail.
They will make a carousel of love.

DAY FOURTEEN

Write a san san, a seven-line poem that rhymes in the pattern
a-b-c-a-b-d-c-d.

Another prompt about what poetic form to use – this time ridicu-
lously complex, involving a lot of half-rhymes, internal rhymes and
words repeated in different locations. I chose as my subject the
trade in sea-otter fur for hats and coats, which was once so popu-
lar that the species was nearly hunted to extinction. They have
the thickest pelt of all animals, with more than a million hairs per
square inch.

I also chose to exercise my right to fudge the rhyme scheme with
slant-rhymes to protect my fraying sanity, which by this stage was
finding complex poetic forms something of an imposition. You
may call it cheating, or even failure; I call it survival.

FUR TRADE

Diving, they are comet-tailed, a plunging silver fizz
of bubbles as the pressure wrings them sleek as fish,
flattening the under-fur that crowds a million to the inch.

One pelagic pelt could mean good silver to the thief
adept to plunge the knife in, to strip the sheath
from vibrissae to tail-tip, so some millionaire can swish
fur-hatted, fizz-swilling through crowds that enviously seethe,
Oh! to wear an otter! it is our dearest aim and wish!

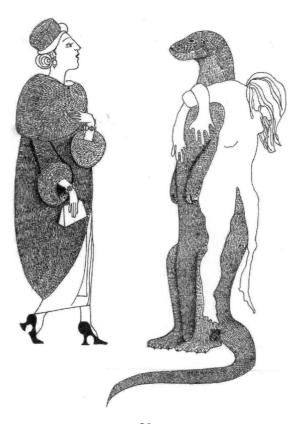

DAY FIFTEEN

Write a poem that incorporates the idea of doubles.

They meant doppelgängers, but I took them a bit more literally, and ludicrously.

DOUBLE THE OTTER

Double the otter is double the fun.
If you could have two, why would you have one?

Double again so your otters are four,
That's eighty sharp claws on your new parquet floor.

But four is no party, let's make it eight,
And if you consider their full-grown weight,

That's almost three hundred and sixty kilos
Of otter, pissing all over the dado.

Imagine the stench when you get to sixteen!
Never again will the hearthrug be clean!

The destruction that one thirty-two-otter raft
Can wreak on a free-standing cast-iron bath!

When the sum of the blighters hits sixty-four,
Flee from the mayhem and move in next door!

Just pray that they don't take up playing bassoon,
This one-hundred-twenty-eight-otter commune –

You may be afflicted by pains existential
If otters keep breeding at rates exponential.

DAY SIXTEEN

Using a series of 'almanac' questions, fill out some details about a real or imagined place. (For example, what are the climate, architecture, local customs like there?) Then write a poem about that place.

I decided to write about Ottery St Mary, which is a real place in Dorset, and which really has a large plughole in the river called the 'Tumbling Weir'. It is also the birthplace of Samuel Taylor Coleridge, famed Romantic poet and opium-eater, so in his honour I fashioned an imagined Ottery, built and inhabited by otters. If you know STC's rather famous poem 'Kubla Khan', you may find my poem a bit familiar…

> *In Xanadu did Kubla Khan*
> *a stately pleasure dome decree…*

(Yep, that's the one.)

IN OTTERY

In Ottery did otter-kind
A wat'ry romping-ground decree
Where through a cunning aperture
Slid the silver'd river pure
Down through the Tumbling Weir.

So culverted and dug about
The river wound both in and out
And there were gardens bright with sinuous rills
Where spawned many a succulent-tasting frog
And here were fish untouched by heron's bills
Plumply fall'n in paws of bitch and dog.

But oh! those muddy chutes that slanted
Down the green banks athwart the tender willows!
A joyous place! as playful and enchanted
As e'er beneath the Hydra's stars was vaulted
By otter leaping in a dwindling oxbow!

And down these mudchutes,
With ceaseless squeals of pleasure,
As if their merriment could last forever,
The otter brethren happily did slide,
Amid whose swift free-spirited glide
The plashy mud did bounce like blessed rain,
And all who slid cried out, 'Again! again!'
And waiting at the bottom, cool as ever
Ran the deep and sacred Otter River.

Five miles meandering with mazy motion
Through wood and dale the sacred river ran,
Diverted from the settlements of man
By otters navigating to the ocean.
Hark, 'cross the waters that they float upon!
Ancestral otters prophesying fun!

There was no shadow in the land of play
Cavorting on the midway of the flow;
All that could be heard by night or day

Were the otters paddling to and fro.
It was a miracle of harmony,
A place where creatures lived so cheerfully!

An otter with a mandolin
I saw once in a waking dream:
It was an Amazonian
And on its mandolin it strummed,
Singing of distant Andes.
Could I revive within me
Its simplicity and song,
To such a deep delight 'twould win me,
That by digging deep and long,
I would build that romping-place,
Those water-slides! That Tumbling Weir!
And all who came should be of cheer,
And all should cry, hooray! hear! hear!
This splashing lark, these waters clear!
Encircle him most utterly
And keep him close unto your hearts
For he has travelled off the charts
To bring us all to Ottery.

DAY SEVENTEEN

Write a poem using a specialist dictionary.

Remarkably like the prompt to use a textbook index, isn't it?
And I wonder why I find it so hard to finish NaPoWriMo. Short
attention span, that's my problem. Where was I? Oh, yes – I
used a Scrabble dictionary, and got all alliterative.

ODE TO THE DIVING OTTER

Observe the otter oscillate
and over-roll, obsidian-wet,
ogive-headed oceanaut,
oligarch of oysterbeds ornate
as origami from the Orient,
his ogee-outline oiltight,
ombré, opalescent.

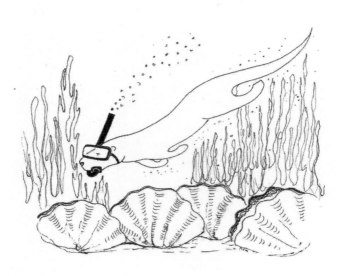

DAY EIGHTEEN

Write a poem that incorporates the 'sound of home' –
dialect, accent, dialogue, family words.

OR, alternatively, remember it's your good friend's birthday and
write an otter poem just for her. And for anyone with a weird
middle name, for example Zooey Deschanel's daughter, who is
called Elsie Otter.

CELEBRITY BABY NAMES

for Nicola Sky Hawkins
and Elsie Otter Pechenik

Celebrities, curb your whimsy
when burdening your child with names
they must struggle to fit, or else outrun.
The Apple may not fall far from the Paltrow,
may yet fulfil all that glossy promise,
but fruit does go bad. Look at Peaches.

Better to slip in a middle name
like a sixpence under a pillow,
a good fairy's cribside blessing,
a seed that may be revealed to the light,
but later, when they choose it,
at the needful point of greatest growth.

A Nicola could punk it up to high-kickin' Nikki,
but what if her mum had tucked away a token
reading 'Sky'? She could kiss it and unfold,
become a thousand times herself more blue
and beautiful when the storms tear through.

Likewise, think of tiny Elsie Pechenik,
who some day may love the granny chic
her name suggests – or hate it; either way,
underneath coy necklines, playful and smart,
she will always know she is Otter at her heart.

DAY NINETEEN

Write a didactic poem that focuses on teaching a particular skill.

I had a great yearning to write something whimsical here, but instead I inadvertently researched the horrific impact of oil spills on sea otters, and wrote my first environmental poem. A different shade of otter.

HOW TO CARE FOR AN OILED OTTER

First, put aside any notion that otters swim,
agile and unblemished, through an ocean
pure as tempered starlight.
Pollute your vision with plastic frags,
run-off, effluent, and the crude suppuration
bleeding out of smashed tankers,
venting from mismanaged seabed hellmouths.
Don't like it? Suck it up.
Tar patties will clog your sentiment until
finally it sinks in – your buoyancy
is fatally compromised.
Now you are ready for the work.

Dip-net for speed, Kevlar-gloved
in case they break open caustic-ravaged mouths to bite,
in case they have some vestige of sight.
Use the stuff-sack, the holding-box, the heat-lamp,
and wash, wash, wash, wash, wash.
Soft water makes a difference. So can you.
For two hours each otter, this is all you do,
care for something that can never
thank you, or profit you, or forgive.
And if their pelage softens and restores its guard,
if their temperature ceases its giddy rollercoaster,
if they have guts enough left unblistered
to digest clams you shuck daily,
if you have used masks and blinds and feeding chutes
so after all of that they are still sufficiently wild,
release them,

and wait for the next time.

DAY TWENTY

Write a poem using the old Norse technique of kennings
– describing an animal, person or object using a two-part
composite word that encapsulates its character or function.
The sea is a 'whale-road', for example.

I have a confession to make. At day twenty, I Hit The Wall. Went
down like a sack of spuds, wept into my cornflakes, just couldn't
write another damn word. Luckily for me, I had written a small
otter poem the year before, so – Reader, I Cheated. It was just a
little wishful thinking from me about actually becoming an otter.
If I were an otter, everything would be better. For example, I
wouldn't have to write a poem every day about otters…

IS IT TOO LATE?

I suppose it's too late to be a sea otter?
To be in some otter place, some sandy inlet
where I may lie back and play a trout harmonica,
swaddled rump to nape in ticklish kelp?

I suppose it's too late to be a god disguised as a sea otter?
To be in some otter time, some golden age
where I might heft my stone abalone-cracker,
teaching men to weigh wisdom heavier than pelts?

DAY TWENTY-ONE

Write a poem from the point of view of a minor character or prop in a fairy-tale or myth.

I combined this with the prompt from day twenty, which I hadn't been able to do due to the aforementioned mental exhaustion/ derangement.

It seemed the perfect time to retell the Norse myth of how Loki killed the otter-magician Ótr, from the point of view of the murder weapon.

THE STONE THAT SLEW THE MAGICIAN OTR

Were I a stone of the road, I would have known to edge away
from the tread of trouble-reaper gods, like all the stones of
Midgard. But I was idling at the river-hem, lazed back on sand.
Like the otter, I was half and half, my belly sun-warming.

I didn't call Loki to reach for me and turn me into a flying axe, I
didn't want to be death for the happy midstream water-tumbler.
Had I voice or breath I would have cried out there and then –

> *That is no more an otter than am I! That frog-chomper*
> *you think to stew, he is shapeshifter, hidden wizard, heir to*
> *power! He is Ótr, and his slayer will pay a heavy price! Loki,*
> *be satisfied with the silver rope of trout now fringing your*
> *shouldered pole, or you'll lose twice that in gold!*

I could not speak. I had no choice but to be the end-blow of
a god's unlucky throw. Bleared and drowned in remorse, I saw
through the glass hall of the river the mighty Ótr skinned, and
the gods depart unwittingly to lay son-flesh on his father's table.
Even this water won't deafen me to the righteous roar to come,
the screams for bloodgold enough to bury a beloved pelt.

So consequences run ahead, for where can Loki find this ransom?
See him, forcing the underwater cave of the dwarf-king! See the
entrance glint coins through the pike-patrolled weeds! See the
future shining with it in fragmentary lights like warning beacons!

Here comes greed, and curses, and the death of lovers.

DAY TWENTY-TWO

Write a poem in honour of Earth Day.

At the time of writing, the peat swamps, mangroves and rainforests of Indonesia were disastrously alight with a man-made blaze. This environmental catastrophe had been wholly, unnecessarily caused by the global palm oil industry, whose derivatives appear in just about every foodstuff and personal hygiene product we use – and I'm sure then as you read this the fires will still be raging. The orang-utans and hairy-nosed otters will still be following the Sumatran tiger into extinction. It will still be impossible to buy toothpaste that doesn't kill the planet.

AN OTTER FOR EARTH DAY

Don't speak to him of tiger economies.
The burnt umber tigers are long-ghosted,

sepia kill-shots snapped where, today, earth burns.
Don't pronounce stearate, octyl palmitate, glycerol.

Doritos matter more than his water snakes.
Lipsticks and instant whip more precious than frogs.

He sprains himself into puddles of peat-swamp,
grieving for mangroves, cool vaulted aquifers.

Acrid, the air bites back. Muzzle-hairs
shake like children locked in nightmares.

My heart, what nasty thing frightened you?
It is coming, it is coming and it won't stop.

DAY TWENTY-THREE

Write a sonnet.
Sometimes they ask questions, then answer them.

Yes, yes, they do, and I was irresistibly drawn to write about the film Ring of Bright Water, whose devastating otter-murder scene made a huge impression on my childhood. Whoops, should I have done a spoiler alert?

RING OF BRIGHT WATER

I ask you now, where did it all go wrong?
When did our innocence first run awry?
Was it when they snipered Bambi's mum,
Making a real stag out of a cutesie-pie?

Or was it with that bloody Bright Eyes song?
Those fuzzy-felt Guevaras of the Down?
Mushroom-tripping myxoma-toasted throng,
That sent the whole Year 6 into a meltdown?

Mine went with a tame otter's scampering run,
The workman raising up his heavy spade,
A sense of fate so forceful that it stunned,
As vivid as the thudding of the blade.

Perhaps it's best for childishness to end –
Wild animals are neither pets nor friends.

DAY TWENTY-FOUR

Write a poem in which two different linguistic registers are mixed.

For me, this meant shuffling very academic, archaic words in amongst some common-as-muck tabloid phrases, all inspired by the Irish Sun's headline 'Devil Otter Ate My Minivan'. Seriously, has there ever been a better news story?

'FARMER ATTACKED BY FURBAG'

A headline the like of which has never since ran,
A shock that that shook us from Spokane to Kazakhstan,
A calumny blathered by a numpty of a man –
'Devil Otter Ate My Minivan'.

It seems that a farmer by the name Joe Burke,
Whilst going about his bucolic work,
Came upon and straight away cornered the creature
Slandered as 'Devil' in the Sun's lead feature.

(This appellation surely was intended to mislead
And manipulate the masses to cough up cash to read,
For otters are peaceable and piscophageous.
To impute Satanic provenance is otterly outrageous.)

Yes, he asserted that he'd sustained a bite,
But we weren't witness, so who knows who is right?
He could be talking out of his welly boots.
Without otter testimony the point is moot.

At the least he showed poverty of judgement
And made himself a target for otterish assailment,
For if a man grabbed your scruff, stuffed you in a sack,
Would you not make petulcous attempts to nut him back?

Having gnawed its way out of one container,
To persist in its escape was a simple no-brainer.
It was the only logical game plan
To eat its way out of the minivan.

So if you catch an otter, don't hold it hostage,
It'll munch through your chassis like a Scot through porridge,
And definitely don't be like that Burke with his van –
Never plug a wild otter's gobhole with your hand.

DAY TWENTY-FIVE

Write a poem that uses as its first line a quote or line from someone else's poem. Use a quote you can remember without looking it up.

Typical me, I could only remember Spike Milligan's 'Can a parrot eat a carrot standing on his head?'

Don't worry, I went with it.

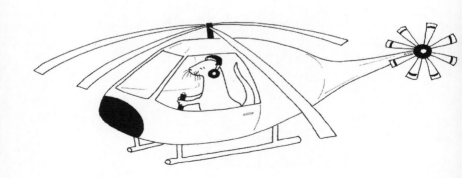

OTTER NONSENSE

Can a parrot eat a carrot standing on his head?
Would a possum scatter blossom on his lover's bed?
Could a peacock dance to bebop if he's in the mood?
Could an otter race a stock car, or would he just get booed?

Can a raven go clean-shaven to evade the law?
Could an emu change a brake shoe on a four-by-four?
Can a lobster be a mobster if he has a gun?
Should an otter be a yachter just to have some fun?

Can an ostrich free the hostage from the terrorists?
Is a weasel on a Nepalese hill scaling Everest?
Could a pigeon get religion if it were brainwashed?
Would an otter tell a whopper, or the truth at any cost?

Can a jackal use block and tackle to raise up a wreck?
Does a donkey wear diamante to the discotheque?
Can a panther be a Morris dancer if he has no rhythm?
If an otter flies a helicopter, must I get in with him?

Can a beaver get Dengue fever sitting in his dam?
A spider in the Large Hadron Collider – does the world go bang?
Would a dolphin and Alec Baldwin have on-screen chemistry?
Are some otters total tossers, or is that only me?

DAY TWENTY-SIX

Write a call-and-response poem.

For this, I imagined a watery congregation of sea otters seeking the blessing of the Inuit goddess of the seas, in all her many forms, praying not to be eaten by a staggering array of sharks...

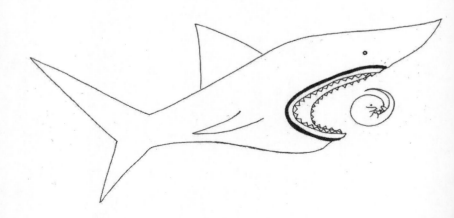

SEA OTTER PRAYER

Sedna, mother of storms,
From Blacktips save us,
From Silvertips, Silkys,
Duskys, Coppers, Blues.
Deliver us safe from their mouths.

Nerrivik, lady of the deep places,
From Tigers keep us,
From Leopards, and Smoothhounds,
Sharptoothed, Grey and Brown.
Deliver us safe from their mouths.

Arnakuagsak, daughter of the creator,
Protect us from Hammerheads,
Malletheads, Bonnetheads,
Bulls, Swells and Sicklefins.
Deliver us safe from their hunger.

Arnapkapfaaluk, Big Bad Woman,
Let us not fall into the Megamouth,
Keep far from us your Goblins,
Horns, Nurses, Pacific Angels.
Deliver us safe from their hunger.

We are the smallest of your fingers
Cut from you and fallen in the bitter sea.
Gather us away from Great Whites.
Sedna, deliver us.

DAY TWENTY-SEVEN

Write a poem with very long lines, at least eleven syllables.

Long lines need long otters, and the longest are the giant otters of the very, very long Amazon river. 'How long are they, Kirsten?' I hear you cry. You'll find out, but only if you reverse my obsessive arithmetic and divide the length of the Amazon by the figure in the last line.

THE PATH OF THE AMAZON IS...

...a dilly-dallying belly-dancer, juggling half-moons hip to hip.

...a slipshod silt-filled seam, stray-dog yellow, stupefied vein of sunlight.

...an unravelled fingerprint, a concertina folded from jaguar tongues.

...a velvet ghost road four million, one hundred and ten thousand otters long.

DAY TWENTY-EIGHT

Write a poem that tells a story backwards.

No.

No, NaPoWriMo, we are nearing the end of this monomaniacal month of mine, and I am feeling mulish. I want to write about the amazing tradition of using trained otters to fish among the mangrove swamps in the Sundarbans, in Bangladesh.

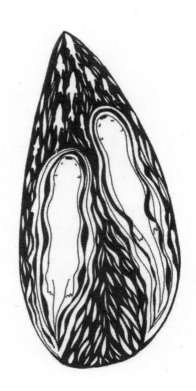

OTTER FISHING IN THE SUNDARBANS

damp-mouthed
the beautiful forest receives
the falling night
smears it kohl-black
along its starless, brackish
watervoids

where fish trace cursive
drowned comets
tinysilvertremblers
elders swung
on the chain of tailflicks
heavy-flanked censers

in a bamboo box
a writhing otterknot
cacophonous yipping
piercing the slats
their whiskers and fetor
of fermented mud

treacherous
the estuaries breath the tide
into their bronchioles
new islands breach
spines of giant crocodiles
midstream, middream

the mud shifts
whispers under
the paws of maneaters
the striped jungle
conceals its secret hives
its weapons
fisherman, release them
longleashed from the narrow boat
dogfaced snouting
fish from crannies

playful, frisking
fish from gullies

in swamps where
translucent women wade
neck-deep dragging
nets through shrimp-seethe
and are eaten tiger-silent
down to their screams

this is the only joyful hunt

DAY TWENTY-NINE

Write an 'I remember' poem.

No. I will write an 'I do not remember' poem.

I will write about the great naturalist and otter enthusiast James Williams, a man I never knew and so do not remember, but who inspired many others to leave stories on his memorial webpage. Please visit www.somersetottergroup.org.uk for information about his life and work.

IN MEMORIAM

I don't remember James, with his cap and stick, and his little laugh.
I don't remember him pushing down the barbed wire and legging over,

trotting back-heeled down the bank to check a turd – dog or otter?
I never ran into him under bridges, peering at dubious dark blobs

on known sprainting rocks, those infamous otter-loos he patrolled.
I don't remember the anatomy of paw-prints he never taught me,

don't think of eels because of him, still have no way to catch crayfish.
When I look at a riverbank, I see only the stones that are visible,

I don't remember to follow my nose along the breeze, across the bend,
I don't remember to see the land like a musk-talker, a scent-dweller.

Never have I bowed at his delicate request to sniff what otters leave –
'a sweet, wild, musky scent of pebbles and water weed and fish

and of the eternal untameable current'. But how I wish I had.

DAY THIRTY

Translate a poem from a language you don't know.

There are no otter poems, at least none we know of, though it is entirely possible they 'write' using urine and musk. But otters, being highly intelligent apex mammals, do use vocalisations. The giant otters of the Amazon have the most distinct 'words' – twenty-two in all, communicating everything from intimacy to hunting directions. This is because they live in the largest social groups, described by some observers as being soap-operatic in their drama and complexity.

However, they absolutely cannot tolerate the proximity of humans; even the noise of nearby human activity stresses them into bizarre and self-destructive behaviours. Reminds me of a lot of student houses I've lived in…

HUMAN-OTTER DICTIONARY

I may not have lived among giant otters,
but I have shared flats
with people I can barely tolerate.
Their hastily-chosen, temporary sexmates,
on catching sight in a door-crack
of my solitary moshing,
have given just that strangled yelp of laughter that would garner a
small dead fish
from an alpha otter momma.

I have beaten wearily at floors and ceilings
in the incoherent Morse of the diurnal trapped among nocturnal
experimental loop-pedallers,
whose weeeekrrrikkering dial-flip zzewstatic WAH interferenzzzzeee
resounded
loud enough to alter the direction
of hunting otter packs
as far afield as Lake Salvador.

I have nursed beers on window seats
whilst macaw-hoarse flirters
swapped throat-back grokkling
in the crowded kitchen,
observed them tsip-tsip their drinks and exit the yikkering, yip-
chuckling party
to 'find a place to be alone'.
Through my wall I have heard them,
little snouty buzzings,
the universal language of purr.

And yes, I have felt that wavering scream of isolation threaten to
come sailing out of me,
like a violin bow dragged ragged on a saw,
though most times I have been considerate, kept the noise down,
at most emitted a pup-squeak
like a balloon dog having its neck wrung.

But no otter ever answers.

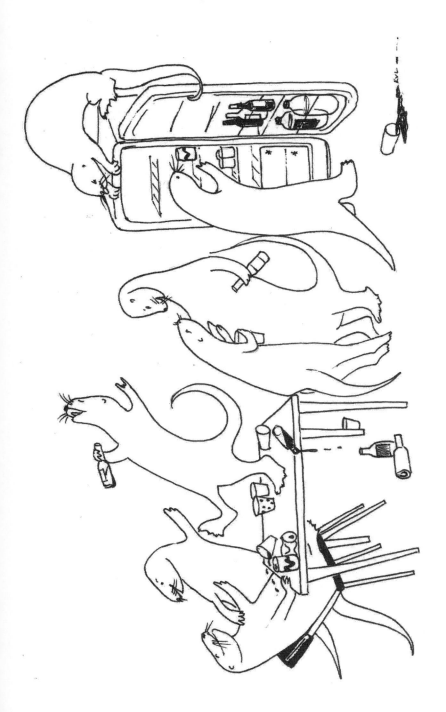

THANKS AND FURTHER READING

I'd like to thank Maureen Thorson, the founder of NaPoWriMo, for giving me permission to namecheck her great project. She'd like you to know that the prompts I've featured were in some cases not written by her, but donated to NaPoWriMo by other generous poets. You can join in every April simply by visiting www.napowrimo.net

To keep an eye on your use of palm oil, you can find shopping guides on www.actforwildlife.org.uk, www.spott.org, www.ethicalconsumer.org or www.worldwildlife.org

You can support conservation work with otters via the International Otter Survival Fund at www.otter.org and the UK Wild Otter Trust at www.ukwildottertrust.org

Thanks go, always, to my Significant Otter, for his steadfast love and support.